AUGUST SNOW

BY REYNOLDS PRICE

★

★

DRAMATISTS
PLAY SERVICE
INC.

AUGUST SNOW
Copyright © 1990, 1989, Reynolds Price

ALL RIGHTS RESERVED

SPECIAL NOTE

For
Rosemary Henenberg
and
Josephine Abady

AUGUST SNOW was first produced as the first part of the trilogy, NEW MUSIC, at the Cleveland Play House (Josephine R. Abady, Artistic Director; Dean R. Gladden, Managing Director), Cleveland, Ohio, on October 10, 1989. It was directed by David Esbjornson; the scene design was by Dan Conway; the costume design was by C.L. Hundley; the lighting design was by John Hastings; the sound design was by Jeffrey Montgomerie; and the production stage manager was Jean Bruns. The cast was as follows:

NEAL AVERY ....Kelly Gwin
TAW AVERY...Susan Knight
ROMA AVERY...Sonja Lanzener
PORTER FARWELL...John Hickey
GENEVIEVE SLAPPY.........................Kathleen Mahony-Bennett

CHARACTERS

NEAL AVERY — age 22, a clerk in Avery's Clothing

TAW AVERY — age 21, Neal's wife and a former school-
teacher

ROMA AVERY — age 43, Neal's mother and a widowed
housewife

PORTER FARWELL — age 22, Neal's best friend and
fellow clerk (his surname is accented on the first syllable:
FAR-well)

GENEVIEVE SLAPPY — age 22, Neal and Taw's landlady,
a lifelong friend of Neal and Porter

TIME AND PLACE

August 1937, a small town in eastern North Carolina.

SCENES

Act One
1. Taw and Neal's room
2. The same
3. Roma's kitchen
4. Taw and Neal's room
5. The Downtown Cafe
6. The same
7. Roma's kitchen

Act Two
1. Genevieve's sitting room
2. The same
3. An alley behind Avery's Clothing
4. The same
5. Roma's kitchen
6. The same
7. Avery's Clothing
8. Taw and Neal's room

AUGUST SNOW

August 1937

Six o'clock in the morning. Clear weak light seeps through the shaded windows of a large one-room apartment — sturdy Victorian oak furniture, a kitchen corner, a wide bedstead, a reclined Morris chair. Taw Avery is asleep in the chair, wrapped in a cotton quilt, her back to the audience.

A door opens silently and Neal Avery enters. Since leaving work the previous evening, he has drunk a great deal of corn liquor; but the only visible hint is a slow gravity in his movements. He walks to the bed and leans on its foot.

Taw has apparently heard nothing.

NEAL. I estimate you will be bent double by New Year's Eve if you spend one more night in that damned chair.
TAW. *(Still not turning but clearly audible.)* Good. I can pick up pennies off the road.
NEAL. Taw, you're out of the orphanage. You married good money — hell, I've rented this grand bed and all these sheets. *(Waves behind him as if Taw can see.)*
TAW. *(Turns and sits up. She is fully dressed in last night's clothes.)* You rent it for *us*, Neal. When you're here, I join you. I promised you that in the only wedding I hope to have. When you vanish, I'd rather sleep cold on the ground.
NEAL. *(Thinks, then shudders and hugs himself.)* I think I slept several hours on the ground since I saw you last.

TAW. *(Rising and moving toward the washstand.)* That's none of my fault. *(Pours water from the pitcher into the bowl and begins to wash her face.)*

NEAL. Never claimed it was. But I'm begging your pardon. *(Taw continues to wash and dry, then to comb her hair. She walks to the kitchen corner — a stove, an old icebox, an enamel dishpan, a water bucket. She takes one egg from a bowl on the shelf, then turns to Neal.)*

TAW. Could you eat a fresh egg if I soft-boil it for you?

NEAL. You never said you pardon me.

TAW. I don't — yet — Neal.

NEAL. Then I couldn't swallow, no. *(Moves to sit on the side of the bed.)* No ma'm, not today.

TAW. You're going to need your full strength today.

NEAL. No ma'm, not for *sleep*. *(Lies back on the bed.)*

TAW. *(Returns the egg to its bowl.)* You can't sleep here. *(When Neal fails to respond, she advances to the table in the midst of the room.)* Don't sleep here, Neal — not today. Please listen.

NEAL. Make it peaceful, Taw.

TAW. I can't. Not now. *(Neal rises to his elbows and faces her, unsmiling.)* This room is all yours, if you plan to claim it. But I'm asking you to leave here now and let us both think through our mess in some kind of calm. *(Sits at the table.)* Neal, I've *thought*. I know what I can do. I can wait here till time for supper this evening. You go off and think about our year together and the time to come. Then if you know I'm the person you need to spend long years with, come back by dark; and I'll start cooking ham and boiling rice.

NEAL. Let me get this plain — you want me to think about what *you* want, the thing you want me to turn into?

TAW. I want you to be a good person, that's all.

NEAL. But *your* good person — a house-broke dog. *(Rises, goes to the table and sits opposite Taw.)*

TAW. *(Waits, then nods.)* House-broke, if that means coming home at sundown to eat and rest — not filthy and sick, not twelve hours late and a good supper ruined, your wife not knowing if you're sick or dead. You *need* to be drunk two or three nights a week? You need to break every promise you made to stand by me?

NEAL. "Forsaking all others"? Did I say that?

TAW. To God and every old lady in town, in the Presbyterian church one evening a whole year ago. I *promised* you, Neal. And you promised me.

NEAL. *(Laughs.)* I was drunk then too.

TAW. No excuse.

NEAL. *(Laughs again.)* I couldn't hear the vows — Porter cried so loud.

TAW. *(Almost smiles.)* You've nearly got a point. Porter should've been shot.

NEAL. No harm in a man's best friend shedding tears when the man takes a wife.

TAW. *(Nods her head slowly as if to agree.)* You sure you took me?

NEAL. It felt like you. You claimed you liked it.

TAW. I liked *you* in it, when you were there and sober. I wouldn't give two cents to do it with any other man alive.

NEAL. How much you give me to do it right now? I'm here and ready.

TAW. *(Studies him, incredulous.)* I paid you, every dollar you cost. I've offered you my whole life to spend.

NEAL. *(Smiles.)* At pretty good interest. On your little terms.

TAW. *(Stands in bafflement, walks to the bed, smooths the wrinkles in the cover, then stands at the foot.)* If loyal attention is little, all right — and keeping your mind clear enough to guide you home in the dark — then sure, I'm one of the littlest dwarfs. *(Neal stands and moves as if to approach her.)* No. Leave like I asked you. If you turn up for supper, on your own two feet and nobody with you, I'll know you want us to keep on together. Otherwise, I'll pack and be gone by morning.

NEAL. Where to?

TAW. There's more than one place for clean young people that are sober round-the-clock and always know their name and address and can be leaned on.

NEAL. You'd die.

TAW. I'd die being true to what I know. *(Neal moves to sit again at the table.)* Please get out. It'll be all yours, one way or an-

9

other, by dark tonight.

NEAL. *(Takes three steps away, turns.)* Should I say goodbye?

TAW. No — well, at least for now. *(Waits.)* I grew up alone. I can't think like you, in a room full of people all joking and mean. Just give me today to think my way clear. You please do the same. Tonight we can cancel goodbye if we're ready.

NEAL. Stop drinking, stop seeing my oldest friend, and be just yours? That's all I've got to decide by supper?

TAW. More or less. It's time.

NEAL. Swear to God, I thought we were doing all right — *I'm* happy.

TAW. I'm not. And you've known it for long months. If not, you're blinder than I ever dreamed. *(Waves slowly around her, the whole still room.)* Neal, I never meant this. I never planned *this.*

NEAL. Taw, you can't plan life.

TAW. You can. I've done it. And it was not *this.*

NEAL. *(Waits, then reaches slowly out in the empty air as if to touch her.)* All right. Goodbye.

TAW. We've got till supper —

NEAL. *(Nods.)* Goodbye. *(Taw gives a small wave. Neal quietly leaves, not looking back.)*

Scene 2

Immediately after Neal's departure, Taw moves to the table and sits in the chair facing the audience. Her speech is an unashamed soliloquy.

TAW. Since I was an orphan so early in life, I taught myself to avoid most dreams — dreams at night, good or bad. They seemed one strain I could spare myself; and I honestly think, in all these years, I've never had two dozen dreams — not to speak of. Neal dreams like a dog by the stove when he's here, the rare nights I get to guard his sleep. Last night though when I finally dozed, sad as I was, I lived through a dream as real as day.

I'd finished my teacher's diploma and was ready to save the world around me, all children. What thrilled me was *that* — they were all young and not too hard yet to help. I'd show them the main thing an orphan knows — how to tuck your jaw and brave hails of pain and come out strong as a good drayhorse or a rock-ribbed house on a cliff by water.

But once I entered my class the first day and trimmed my pencil and faced the desks, I saw they'd given me twenty grown men — all with straight sets of teeth. I prayed I was wrong, that I'd got the wrong room. Still I said my name, and the oldest man at the back of the room stood tall at last in a black serge suit and said "Don't wait another minute to start. We've paid our way."

I had a quick chill of fright that I'd fail; but then I thought of the week they died — my mother and father, of Spanish flu — and I knew I did have a big truth to tell, the main one to know.

I opened my mouth and taught those grown men every last fact an orphan needs and learns from the day she's left — courage and trust and a craving for time. They listened too but hard as I looked in all the rows, I never saw Neal.

Scene 3

Immediately after. The kitchen of Roma Avery, Neal's mother — an out-of-date but tidy room: late Victorian oak furniture (a table and chairs, a sizable rocker), adequate electrical appliances and other cooking gear of the time. Porter Farwell stands at the range, scrambling eggs. He is dressed for work, his jacket on a chair; but he cooks with unhurried competence, no wasted moves.

Roma enters in nightgown and bathrobe.

Porter does not hear her.

ROMA. You're taking kitchen privileges, I see.

PORTER. *(Surprised.)* Oh yes ma'm. I didn't see any point in calling you.

ROMA. And no point either in not telling me you planned not to spend last night in your room? I barely shut an eye.

PORTER. By the time I knew where I'd be, it was too late to call.

ROMA. Porter, cast your mind back. I rented you Neal's room the day he left so I wouldn't lie here helpless at night to any passing felon.

PORTER. Let me fix you some of my feather-light eggs.

ROMA. Just coffee please. *(Roma sits at the head of the table. Porter serves Roma coffee, then brings his own plate of eggs and sits at her right.)*

PORTER. Mrs. Avery, I'd bet a day's pay you were truly the only eye open in town after midnight.

ROMA. Half the world's rapes are over by midnight.

PORTER. I won't doubt your word. I know how hard you've researched the subject. *(Begins to eat.)*

ROMA. Porter, recall I'm much your elder and a recent widow. Show some respect. *(Tastes the coffee, frowns hard but continues drinking.)* Since I was the only soul awake, where was your sleepy head? And my son's, may I ask?

PORTER. You asked us to check on your dogs, remember?

ROMA. The hounds of the Dear Departed, not mine.

PORTER. He'd be pleased to see how well they've done.

ROMA. He'd be mad as hell. Britt Avery hoped we'd all roll round — dogs included — prostrate with grief, ever after he died.

PORTER. Well, the dogs are grand — not one tearful eye. Of course, old Turner doesn't hunt them enough. They're plump as ladies and doze all day. They've hatched a few puppies — you own sixteen fine fox-dogs today.

ROMA. You and Neal better hunt them to the bone this fall; or I plan to give one each, in person, to the first sixteen honest children I meet in the road.

PORTER. How will you know the honest ones?

ROMA. *(Studies her face in the back of a spoon.)* I'll ask them to describe my looks in five words. Anybody not saying "Ugly as

12

a scalded rabbit" *(Counts the words on her fingers.)* gets no hound dog.

PORTER. Mrs. Avery, you forget we married Neal off. Now we've got to help him put away childish things.

ROMA. *(Takes up a large salt shaker, slowly unscrews the top.)* And sit down in one rented room, no private bath, while Miss Taw Sefton preaches her sermons on true love and virtue?

PORTER. She's Mrs. Neal Avery now, for some reason.

ROMA. Ask her; ask Taw — she'll tell you all day and into the night. *Neal* could no more tell you than this salt could. *(Ceremoniously empties the shaker into her palm — a damp teaspoon of salt — then shuts her fingers on it.)*

PORTER. He *wants* her, right now.

ROMA. *(Rises, moves toward the sink.)* Then stand back; it's love.

PORTER. Ma'm?

ROMA. You just defined *love* — hot need, right *now.*

PORTER. Then anybody's love can end any day.

ROMA. *(Brushes salt from her hand.)* I think you'll find that's a fact about love they don't advertise.

PORTER. I doubt I believe you.

ROMA. Then don't grow up. *(Neal stands in the door. Porter senses him and turns; they nod, unsmiling.)*

PORTER. *(To Roma.)* Your wandering boy's hungry.

ROMA. *(Not facing Neal.)* He's not mine now.

NEAL. You're dead-wrong — I'm not a bit hungry. But Mother, I'm yours.

ROMA. Try the Salvation Army.

PORTER. Sit here; you're pale. I saved you some eggs. *(Porter stands and goes to the oven for eggs. Neal walks to his mother, kisses her neck. Then he sits in her place at the head of the table. Porter serves him while Roma stands to watch.)*

ROMA. *(As Neal takes the first mouthful.)* That's *my* chair.

NEAL. It was Father's, then mine.

ROMA. *(Moving toward him.)* And both of you quit it. *(Stands at Neal's side. Neal rises and moves his plate beyond Porter, then quietly sits. Roma sits again and smiles.)* Thank you, son.

NEAL. I may reclaim it.

ROMA. *(Laughs.)* It would have to be earned. *(All turn for a*

moment to their plates and cups.)
PORTER. You fix things at home?
NEAL. Taw's all right. *(They eat and drink again.)*
ROMA. I haven't heard the rest of where you laid those two clever heads last night. I mean, after you'd seen my big fat dogs — not at Taw's, I take it. *(Porter looks first to Neal, then gestures toward him.)*
NEAL. Mother, you'll live years longer not knowing.
ROMA. My people live *far* into their nineties. I've been wife to a half-mute skinflint, mother to a souse; and now I'm heir to a men's clothing store that's showing a profit for the first year in ten. So sure, hit me hard; I doubt I'll break.
NEAL. *(To Porter.)* How much have you told her?
PORTER. Just the dogs.
NEAL. Old Turner, you can guess, has time on his hands — his wife and mother-in-law do the farming, and his girl feeds the dogs. So when we got there, he had just finished making a dugout canoe — burnt from a cypress log and lovely as somebody's neat strong leg.
   You know I've wanted one all my life; so I offered him five dollars for it, on the spot. He moaned and bragged for half an hour, then took eight dollars and my old nailclippers in exchange for something even you would love. *(Pauses to eat.)*
ROMA. *(Pleased now and beginning to warm.)* Where is it?
NEAL. Porter, where is it?
PORTER. In thick honeysuckle near where you slept. I hid it at dawn.
NEAL. *(To Roma.)* We took it to the river to test.
ROMA. In night black as Egypt?
NEAL. Porter, was it dark? Yes ma'm, must have been — way past suppertime. We drove to the sandbar and slid the boat in. Funny, I remember it all as daylight — good sharp pictures. Then we just drifted down with the current — what, Porter? — maybe two miles, past that rock your father used to skin otters on.
ROMA. My great-grandfather. No otter round here for eighty-odd years.
NEAL. Porter, weren't you singing every inch of the way?

14

PORTER. No sir, I was too busy praying not to drown.

NEAL. Never one minute's danger. I could balance on a web, much less the Brown River. And a little past the rock is that notch in the bank with the crippled tree. I landed us there, safe as Captain Cook.

ROMA. Captain Cook was slaughtered in the Sandwich Islands by tattooed natives.

NEAL. I imitate his *better* days. Then we slept — right, Porter?

PORTER. You did, after telling me more than I planned about your honeymoon and other old jokes. I was mainly awake, keeping guard against wolves.

NEAL. Hasn't been a wolf around here since Columbus.

ROMA. Since I was a girl.

PORTER. We're all safe now — send silver donations in lieu of thanks to Porter Farwell.

ROMA. *(Smiles.)* You'll hear from my lawyer. *(To Neal.)* And son, I believe you left out the corn.

NEAL. Beg your pardon?

ROMA. Corn liquor. I figure you bought some liquor from Turner and floated that boat and yourselves on corn.

NEAL. Goes without saying.

ROMA. It killed my father.

NEAL. Your father was shot at the wrong back door.

PORTER. Drunk as a goat in love, at the time.

ROMA. Porter, eat your sausage. This is family business. *(Porter laughs but obeys. To Neal.)* If Miss Taw Sefton drives you to drink, then seize the wheel back. You come from far too long a line of sots.

NEAL. Mother, notice I'm bound to the former Taw Sefton. *(Holds up his ring finger, a single gold band.)*

ROMA. Gold will melt in a fire.

PORTER. Whoa! *(Laughs edgily and stands.)* Time for work. I mean to go wash my mouth out with soap; you both do the same. *(Sets his dishes in the sink and goes to the door.)* Neal, meet you on the porch in three minutes, hear? *(Leaves. Neal nods, not looking. Roma stands and moves more plates to the sink. From there she changes her tone.)*

15

ROMA. Son, once you've opened up, call me from the store. We need to talk about winter hats.

NEAL. *(Faces round in his chair, nods, stands.)* This'll be a long day.

ROMA. Eat lunch with me?

NEAL. *(Steps toward the door.)* I'd better not, thank you.

ROMA. Taw coming to meet you?

NEAL. Not today. Got a lot on my mind.

ROMA. Be good to your mind. It started life smart. I know; I made you.

NEAL. *(Smiles and shrugs.)* All right, all right. I won't fight you now. *(Neal stands in place a moment, intending his concession to be the last word. But Roma takes two steps forward and shakes her head.)*

ROMA. No. Don't. *(Neal thinks, then slowly turns, pauses at a shelf and mirror by the door and brushes his hair. Then he leaves. Roma steps to the table and flicks at crumbs.)*

Scene 4

Just before noon, Taw and Neal's rented room. Taw is freshly dressed, her hair combed neatly, and is taking clothes from a tall wardrobe, rehanging some but choosing others to fold and lay in squared-off piles on the bed. It's a melancholy chore and the imminent chance of real heartbreak marks all her acts, even in the face of her visitor's encouragement.

A knock at the door.

Taw hesitates but unlocks and opens on Genevieve Slappy, their resident landlady, in uncombed hair and housecoat.

TAW. You're up early, Genevieve. It's barely noon.

GENEVIEVE. If I slept fifteen minutes all night, I sure don't recall.

TAW. *(Stepping aside to wave her in.)* I do — you *did.* *(Points to the ceiling.)* Those hairline cracks in the plaster there? You snore in earnest. *(Locks the door.)*

GENEVIEVE. *(Moves toward the icebox.)* No such thing. I prayed the whole time. You got any chocolate pudding left? *(Pats the top of the icebox, not touching the door.)*

TAW. I ate the last spoonful at four a.m. *(Returns to the bed and again sorts clothes.)*

GENEVIEVE. You don't plan to ask what kept me awake?

TAW. Gen, the whole population south of Boston knows who worries you.

GENEVIEVE. *(Laughs.)* No such thing — I *hide* my wounds. Who woke you at four?

TAW. Nobody. *Nobody.*

GENEVIEVE. Neal never showed up.

TAW. You asking or telling? *(Smiles.)* Either case, you're wrong. He showed his drunk face just after dawn.

GENEVIEVE. That's a good deal more than Wayne Watkins showed.

TAW. Wayne is not your husband.

GENEVIEVE. He wants to be.

TAW. Then who please is stopping him?

GENEVIEVE. Don't be mean, Taw. It spoils your skin.

TAW. Help yourself to the rest of the peach pie and sit. *(Genevieve opens the icebox, takes out the pie plate, locates a fork, then sits at the central table to eat.)*

GENEVIEVE. Where had he been now, and what was his story?

TAW. Under the stars with you-know-who, I guess. I didn't ask. I don't trust myself not to break any minute.

GENEVIEVE. You're as likely to break as the pyramids at Giza. When you hold Neal Avery to the line is when you'll *know.*

TAW. Know what?

GENEVIEVE. How much of a life you'll have, from here on.

TAW. A damned sight better life than I've had *this* year — you and Wayne upstairs shredding the rafters while I sat here praying Porter Farwell would return my spouse to these empty arms with no parts missing, as daylight broke.

GENEVIEVE. I apologize for Wayne and me.

TAW. That's not the point. You don't bother me.

GENEVIEVE. The hell it's not. The whole point is how to live

close to human beings and not get killed, not kill one of them. *(Waits and wonders if she has pushed too far.)*
I didn't plan to say it; but I've lived some, believe me — with more than just Wayne — and Taw, the *point* is what you've missed all along.

TAW. And you see it plainly?

GENEVIEVE. Yes ma'm, I do — to my own heartbreak.

TAW. *(Suddenly turning to sit on the bed, among her own clothes.)* I bet I can guess — two good short mottoes, suitable for stitching: Living Alone Is Worse Than Being Dead; Bear Any Grade of Hell Your Mate Needs to Hand You.

GENEVIEVE. *(Positively.)* You can laugh now. I pray you never know first-hand what I know.

TAW. You're what — one whole year older than me? So don't try sounding all-wise yet. And *alone* I'd have to swear, if called to court, that Wayne Watkins spends more time here than daylight.

GENEVIEVE. Be ashamed. *(But she smiles.)* You're wasting too much time as a spy.

TAW. Then get me another job — Neal won't let me teach.

GENEVIEVE. You could start by asking where you've gone wrong to cause a good boy — that I *know's* kind and true — to plow up the world just to prove he's sad. I'm your friend till the devil reclaims me, but I have to say this — Neal used to be happy. People welcomed his face.

TAW. I could welcome him today. *(Rises from the bed, goes to the dining table and slowly sits.)* Understand, I'm *proud* to claim I'm the main cause of all this mess he makes. He's run up finally against one human that asks him to give her the best he's got and won't take less.

GENEVIEVE. You're proud of that?

TAW. A little, yes. And Gen, Neal *wanted* it. He knew me two years before he chose me. He knew I couldn't stand a life like this.

GENEVIEVE. And you knew him, knew he was wild in a harmless way — getting tight, taking jaunts for days on end to see some sight in the mountains or a baseball game on donkey-back. More than one person thought Neal killed his father with

18

undue worry but I never did.

His daddy had Roma Avery on his back — she's known to be healthy as a sack of rat-bait. And everybody knew God above tended Neal — Neal's driven off roads into sheer ravines more times than I've made first-class fudge.

TAW. Not with me he hasn't.

GENEVIEVE. Pity on you; you missed a good time. *(Waits, then tentatively.)* I told you about the time we had to get the Lightning Calculator to drive us home, didn't I?

TAW. Us?

GENEVIEVE. *(Nods.)* Wayne and I — we were in on some of Neal's best adventures. See, one day Miss Boyd, our algebra teacher, read out a long piece from the paper saying they had this lame boy in Windy, near the mountains; and the boy could watch a whole freight train pass, add up in his head the serial number on the side of each car, then give you the total at the sight of the caboose. He was ten years old and was already called the Lightning Calculator up that way.

I listened and promptly forgot the story. But Saturday night of the same week, we were all at a dance. Most of the boys had already, so to speak, blurred their vision; and I was thinking I might walk home again — my bosoms had finally blossomed, so I wasn't eager to risk harming *them.*

But Neal stepped up — "I'm leaving in a minute for Windy, N.C. I plan to spend Sunday with the Lightning Calculator. Who's coming along?"

Before I could scuttle and strike out for home, Wayne said "I am, me and Genevieve Slappy" — he still likes to use my awful name, however mad it makes me. Before I could breathe, much less say No, we were on the damned highway. All I could do was pray for life and the prayers worked.

TAW. Was the boy awake?

GENEVIEVE. *Awake?* He was fully dressed and on the porch at daybreak. Neal walked right up and asked when the next freight train was due. Without one word of "Who are you?" or "Go to hell," the Lightning Calculator said "An hour." His real name was Jarvis, Sylvester Jarvis.

His mother appeared at the screen door then and said

"Vester, who's all this so early?" Next thing you knew we were eating fried apples and drinking coffee strong enough to ream a radiator.

TAW. Neal was sober by then?

GENEVIEVE. For an hour or two — that's the *end* of the story.

TAW. I may not last.

GENEVIEVE. Do. It's the happy part. *(Taw nods and smiles but rises quietly, goes to the wardrobe and resumes her work.)* It turned out Vester was eleven not ten, but the lame part was true. His left leg was bowed like the big-letter *C*, and he rolled when he walked. So just before seven he rolled us all back out to the porch, and here came the freight on a fast downgrade.

I could barely see the numbers on the cars, but Sylvester's lips were working top-clip. Neal had squatted beside him. When the last car passed, the child stood up and said "Fourteen million, two hundred twenty thousand and seventy-six."

Wayne and I were speechless with wonder. But Neal just stayed at Vester's bad knee and said "Son, who in the world can *check* you?" Vester gazed off toward a mountain and swallowed. Even the newspaper hadn't caught on. There was nobody fast enough to check the child's total. He could just have been estimating or lying.

TAW. Did Vester fight back?

GENEVIEVE. Not a word. I think he was somehow relieved to be caught. The Lightning Calculator was dead; now he could go on and be just a child. But he shed a few tears. When Wayne said "Lightning, *I* still believe you," Vester turned round and his cheeks were wet. So out of the wild blue, Neal said "Ace, I bet you can drive." Vester thought a minute and then said "Yeah, I like that name." Neal of course called him *Ace* the whole way home.

TAW. He didn't come with you?

GENEVIEVE. Sugar, Ace *drove* us every mile of the way. We were all asleep, trusting as babes.

TAW. Did his mother know?

GENEVIEVE. Knew and made three dollars on the deal. Neal gave her that much as we drove off; and he sent Ace home on the evening train with a brand-new hacksaw over his shoulder, which was all he wanted by way of a present.

TAW. I guess he's gone on to rob trains and banks.

GENEVIEVE. *(Waits.)* That wasn't my point, Taw, I'm sad to say.

TAW. *(Smiles.)* Write it out then and mail it to me.

GENEVIEVE. Neal's – a – funny – kind – soul.

TAW. Why did *you* pass him up?

GENEVIEVE. I've loved a lot of people, but I just wanted Wayne. *(Laughs.)* And of course I never got a chance at Neal.

TAW. May have been the best luck you'll ever have. *(Genevieve waits, then rises slowly and walks to Taw. When they are face to face, both unsmiling, Genevieve puts out a gentle hand and covers Taw's mouth.)*

GENEVIEVE. Take that back right now while you can. *(Genevieve retracts her hand. Taw shakes her head No. The hall door rattles; someone tries to enter. Silence, then a knock, then Neal's voice.)*

NEAL. Taw — *(Genevieve's hand goes up for a second touch at Taw's mouth. But Taw steps back, shakes her head No harder. Then she moves to the door, turns the key and opens it. Neal is still in yesterday's clothes; but his face is clean, his hair brushed down.)*

TAW. You found a hairbrush at least.

NEAL. I stopped by home.

TAW. Where is that?

NEAL. *(Points.)* My mother's.

TAW. Then what's this room? *(Neal steps past her and smiles at Genevieve. Genevieve gives a little-girl curtsey in reply.)*

NEAL. *(Turns back to Taw.)* This is the room we rented from my friend Genevieve Slappy to start our life.

GENEVIEVE. And Genevieve's leaving. Enjoy your lunch. *(Genevieve steps briskly to the door. Neal sees the stacks of clothes on the bed and goes to touch them. Genevieve whispers goodbye to Taw. Taw shuts the door behind her, not locking it now. Neal lifts up a cardigan sweater of Taw's and holds it before him.)*

NEAL. You having a sale?

TAW. No.

NEAL. *(Holds up a single arm of the sweater, clasps the body to him and dances two steps.)* Inventory?

TAW. I told you I might have to pack tonight — so, sure, *inventory.* All of it's mine. *(Facing Taw, Neal folds the sweater neatly, then suddenly collapses backward on the bed. Taw makes a startled move to help him but stops by the table.)*

NEAL. *(Still flat.)* Then pack for me too.

TAW. Is that your answer?

NEAL. *(Sits upright.)* It just may be.

TAW. *(Sits at the table.)* No may-bes now.

NEAL. Then no, I haven't answered.

TAW. If I pack us both, we'll be gone for good. We'd leave here tonight — go someplace and breathe.

NEAL. *(Takes a long breath.)* I'm not short of air.

TAW. We're strangling, Neal.

NEAL. Who's twisting *your* rope?

TAW. *Our* rope — you know well as me.

NEAL. Mother.

TAW. She's half.

NEAL. Not Porter.

TAW. Porter Farwell.

NEAL. *(Waits, then firmly.)* I can't stop knowing my oldest best friend.

TAW. That's part of what every marriage is for — bury your dead and make a clean start. You love too many people.

NEAL. That's easy enough for an orphan to say.

TAW. *Shame* and you know it — I'd walk through streaming lava right now for my Aunt Jess.

NEAL. That's where we're going? — Hawaii? Fresh lava?

TAW. *(Refuses the bait.)* Don't talk that trash — you know what I mean. But you come first, a long way first.

NEAL. You do for me, from the time I saw you.

TAW. That day at the horseshoe match, when you won?

NEAL. *(Stands, goes to the window and faces out.)* I saw you maybe two months before that.

TAW. Never told *me.*

NEAL. A lot I never told you, maybe never will. *(Waits.)* But I sure God saw you, naked as a peeled pear, drying your arm — among other parts.

TAW. Don't tell that lie.

NEAL. I climbed a tree to see you — nearly broke my neck.

TAW. *(Smiles.)* Must have been the day Miss Ella washed the curtains. She told me not to bathe. *(Waits.)* I hope you were alone.

NEAL. *(Nods.)* Creeping home alone. Saw the top of Miss Taw Sefton's head and took the dare.

TAW. It can't have been worth it.

NEAL. *(Smiles.)* I'll know someday. Right now I've just got a picture in my mind — you upright in that foggy bathroom with no other pair of hands to take and keep you. I thought I'd volunteer.

TAW. You waited long months.

NEAL. You weren't on the run.

TAW. Some other Peeping Tom could have beat you to me.

NEAL. I figured I'd win.

TAW. Stuck-up — think you did?

NEAL. Till this morning, yes.

TAW. And now you've lost?

NEAL. *(Moves from the window halfway to Taw.)* I may have, yes.

TAW. *(Rises in place at the table.)* I hope not.

NEAL. I believe you. *(Moves toward the door and opens it slowly.)*

TAW. Take till tonight — *(Neal faces her intently but does not speak or give a sign.)* You want me to wait?

NEAL. *(Calm but firm.)* You've decided everything else here today. *(Taw moves a step toward him. But Neal turns and leaves.)*

Scene 5

One-thirty in the afternoon. Porter sits at a table in the Downtown Cafe, finishing lunch.

Neal enters, locates Porter and joins him.

PORTER. It's getting late. I started without you. Any change to report?

NEAL. *(Waits.)* Let's leave that alone — my brain is *fried.* *(Porter nods and watches Neal closely. Waits.)* I guess I ought to just bunk at Mother's till Taw calms down, but with you up there —

PORTER. Neal understand this — I'm not determined to live at your mother's; she and I are not some secret team out to drive you off.

NEAL. *(Nods.)* I didn't think so.

PORTER. But if you're hunting space, it is a big house. I'll move out of your room the instant you want it. With ten minutes' notice, we can move me downstairs.

NEAL. The sewing room?

PORTER. I'm a pretty fair seamster.

NEAL. Those models of Mother's bust through the years wouldn't rile your sleep?

PORTER. Take more than any lady's bosom to wake me, tired as I am today.

NEAL. Don't worry about it, tonight anyhow. If I sleep at Mother's, I'll flop on the sofa till my plans congeal. Anything worth eating?

PORTER. *(Glancing at the plate.)* Chicken dumplings, green peas and biscuits. They've got fish too. You need to eat.

NEAL. I doubt I'm hungry. Hell, I don't know *anything* I want.

PORTER. *(Waits and then, in full awareness of the dare he takes, leans forward.)* I know what *I* want, every day from now on.

NEAL. Is it something I should hear?

PORTER. *(Halting, the first confession of his life.)* I figured you knew, had known all your life. Some version of last night — a dugout, a river, deep night, you asleep.

NEAL. You awake, on guard?

PORTER. *(Sits back, laughs, finds his answer slowly.)* Something like that. Crazy. And practical as — snowshoes — in August — in Mexico.

NEAL. I think they have mountains in Mexico where snow never melts.

PORTER. Hope they do. But this is Carolina. People go barefoot eight months a year.

NEAL. And stand stock-still in place all their lives. *(Waits.)* Unless there's a war.

PORTER. After 1918, a *world* war's out. And the South won't rise.

NEAL. You don't know that; you read it somewhere. There's millions of square miles we've never seen. You and I've traveled more than anybody near; and where have we been? — north to Richmond, east to Nags Head, west far as Windy, no farther south than Charleston.

PORTER. I'm no big explorer.

NEAL. But you're miserable here.

PORTER. Not me, no.

NEAL. You had me fooled. I thought that was liquor you poured down your gullet. You drink more than me.

PORTER. I drink *with* you. You've begged me to.

NEAL. That's a pitiful reason.

PORTER. It's mine. I like it.

NEAL. Shame *on* you then.

PORTER. All right.

NEAL. *(Waits.)* No wonder we're stuck; we've just been too damned lazy to run..

PORTER. You forgot your feet.

NEAL. Sir?

PORTER. Your two flat feet. Armageddon could come; you'd never get drafted, not with those feet.

NEAL. Forget my feet. I own four horses. And the car's been invented — we could head on south. We've never seen Texas. Hell, a Model A can drive in Spanish as fast as English.

PORTER. Faster. *(Waits.)* When we get there — what? We can't *work* in Spanish.

NEAL. You're rich; you're the one with the big nest egg.

PORTER. Big enough to see us far as Social Circle, Georgia and buy us one fried-oyster dinner apiece.

NEAL. *(Serious.)* I may want that.

PORTER. From now on out? Till Hell comes calling?

NEAL. *(Waits.)* I'm too tired to choose, at least right now.

PORTER. *Now's* what you've got, to choose Taw at least. Me and Mexico or down on the river might wait awhile longer.

NEAL. *(Calm.)* For me? All my life?

PORTER. I've answered that, Neal — most days you've known me.

NEAL. *(Watches Porter, then firmly.)* Every livelong day. *(Porter*

sits a moment, facing Neal; then stands in place and consults his pocket watch.)
PORTER. *Late* here, boy. May lose my job.
NEAL. *(Stands, serious.)* I'll speak to the boss. *(Porter hurries out.)*

Scene 6

Immediately after. As Porter leaves, Neal turns back slowly, moves far downstage and faces the audience. As he speaks he gradually retreats; by the end he is far upstage, marooned.

NEAL. One thing I know I'm not is conceited. So believe what I say, in this one respect. The trouble, my whole life, has been this — people fall for me, what they *think* is me. They mostly call it love, and it generally seems to give them fits. They think life can't go on without me — when I know life can go on in the dark if they blind you, butcher you down to a torso, stake you flat on a rank wet floor and leave you lonesome as the last good soul.

Neal Avery can't save the *shrubbery* from pain, much less human beings. It may be the reason I act so bad to Taw and my mother and Porter, my friend. It may be why I'm soaked to the ears so much of the time — *I know I'm me,* an average white boy with all his teeth, not Woodrow Wilson or Baby Jesus or Dr. Pasteur curing rabies with shots.

Who on God's round Earth do they think I am? Who would patch their hearts up and ease their pain? If I stand still here for many years more, won't they wear me away like the Sphinx or a doorsill, just with the looks from their famished eyes?

If I wasn't a Methodist, if this wasn't home, wouldn't I be well advised to strip and run for the nearest desert cave and live among wolves or crows or doves? Wouldn't they simply elect me gamekeeper?

Am I ruined past help? Could I take ten steps on my own — here to there — much less flee for life, for my good and theirs?

26

Scene 7

Two in the afternoon, Roma Avery's kitchen. Roma is napping in a large rocker, a thick book open facedown in her lap.

Taw climbs the steps to the front door and knocks.

Roma wakes, frowning, and slowly moves to answer. At the sight of Taw, Roma waits in silence, smiling.

TAW. I know it's your nap time.

ROMA. *(Still smiling.)* Wrong, Mrs. Avery. I seldom bat an eye — *(Waves Taw in.)* Just pause once a day to think great thoughts. You must be collecting for a desperate cause.

TAW. Why's that?

ROMA. To call on me, alone, here in daylight. Who are the starving Armenians this time?

TAW. The Averys.

ROMA. Not *this* Avery. I ate two drumsticks for lunch and peach cobbler.

TAW. I haven't had a morsel since yesterday.

ROMA. Sit down. I'll tend to that.

TAW. I came for something else.

ROMA. *(A long wait.)* Sit anyhow and tell me. *(Roma returns to her chair, takes her book up and sits again. Taw goes to an opposite chair but stands beside it. Roma holds up the book.)* Read this yet?

TAW. No ma'm. I —

ROMA. You better! It's had me stroking my knee all week. Anything'll make me touch this body is bound to be good.

TAW. Your body's all right, Mrs. Avery.

ROMA. For glue. Some days I think I'll walk myself, while I still have steam and can see the road, to the nearest glue factory.

TAW. *(Smiles.)* Wait a few years.

ROMA. You speaking for yourself or Neal or who?

TAW. Oh, the general populace. You know — most of us.

ROMA. Sit down please. You're lying. You never liked me. *(Taw, to her own surprise, sits. With unusual care she settles her skirt and jacket.)*

TAW. Yes ma'm, I did — once or twice, when your rough edge showed.

ROMA. Like now? *(Taw extends a hand as if to halt a charge. Roma waits, then nods.)*

TAW. I didn't come here to fight.

ROMA. All right if you did.

TAW. I wouldn't know how.

ROMA. The hell you wouldn't. You took my one child off and broke him. *(Though she nearly conceals it, Taw is stunned. No one else has struck as hard as this. Roma searches Taw's face, then continues in the same level voice.)* I'm sorry. I'm cursed with telling the truth. Neal's father used to say "Roma, trouble with you is, you're a *truth* monger."

TAW. Neal told me that.

ROMA. It's nothing I'm proud of.

TAW. *(Nods.)* I wondered.

ROMA. Last thing people want, especially your kin.

TAW. I want it now. *(Waits.)* How have I broken Neal?

ROMA. You married him.

TAW. That was his idea as much as mine.

ROMA. More so, I'm sure — men invented mistakes. That didn't mean you had to compound it by climbing aboard, all smiles in bushels of satin and veil. Neal was smothered by the time the last note sounded.

TAW. Mrs. Avery, marriage is the way people live.

ROMA. Some few do, yes — the saints of the Earth. It fells most others in a few quick weeks, right dead in their tracks — still grinning like dogs from the wedding reception.

TAW. Then what are people meant to do about love?

ROMA. *(Smiles.)* Ah *love*. Comes in more than one color and size. People want their knees, and elsewhere, stroked — every week or so. No problem with that; just ask somebody and pull down the shades. Or your neighbors and God — keep fresh cakes handy, visit the sick and send up thankful prayers once a day. I pray at dawn; I'm more thankful then.

TAW. Don't mock me please.

ROMA. I'm not. Sit back. I haven't got to you.

TAW. I need to get home.

ROMA. You *do*. But I'll just take another minute. *(Waits.) Love.* You and Neal. The smoky kind — two months of fire, a year of coals, decades of smoke. You've either got to stand still and learn to breathe smoke or leave here alone, get your hands red with scandal and hope to live it down.

TAW. Or leave here tonight — Neal and I both, just the clothes on our backs. Leave you and Porter and the pitiful job, this dreadful house — and watch the smoke clear, all on its own.

ROMA. *(Not visibly fazed.)* Speak for you, Taw — *you*. Neal Avery lives *here*. *(Leans forward slowly and points to the floor.)*

TAW. I believe you.

ROMA. Blow me down!

TAW. I believe Neal dreams he still lives here. I'm finally asking you to help me wake him up.

ROMA. And that means telling him goodbye forever and crouching up here to die alone?

TAW. You're a young strong woman.

ROMA. Strong enough to fight.

TAW. And nobody ever leaves anyone *forever*, not their mother at least.

ROMA. *(Smiles, shakes her head.)* No ma'm, every day. Don't you know that's the founding faith of America? — leave your poor old mother in her cold sod hut and strike out with some pretty thing for freedom: Ellis Island — Oklahoma.

TAW. *(Waits.)* I've asked Neal to leave, with me — to anywhere.

ROMA. What's his answer?

TAW. None yet. He's got till tonight.

ROMA. To tell you whether he'll leave or not?

TAW. And stop drinking liquor with Porter Farwell till he drops in ditches.

ROMA. *(Smiles.)* You packed?

TAW. Yes.

ROMA. For you *and* Neal?

TAW. Just me, till tonight.

ROMA. What happens tonight?

TAW. Neal tells me his plan.

ROMA. Neal can't plan tying his shoes and you know it.

TAW. *(Nods.)* He's learning right now. He's got till dark.

ROMA. *(Laughs.)* Dark in what century — the twenty-third?

TAW. No ma'm. Now. He knows I won't wait.

ROMA. You said you could. I sat in church in a fine lace dress and heard you vow — cost me thirty-five dollars and it's hot as Bombay. I won't haul that out, ever again. You and Neal are *stuck*.

TAW. Not me, not for long. If Neal won't honor the vows we took, then he sets me free.

ROMA. You believe in freedom, this side of the grave?

TAW. I have to, yes.

ROMA. You think you've ever seen it? Show me a sample.

TAW. *(Waits, then slowly shakes her head.)* You'd sit here and mock it.

ROMA. I'd weep for joy. I've waited long years.

TAW. I hope Neal and I can end your vigil.

ROMA. How so?

TAW. With a serious life together, wherever we go. Real love is freedom — two people free to choose but choosing each other, day by day.

ROMA. God help you, child.

TAW. He already has. He's guiding me now.

ROMA. *(Studies her, bemused.)* I can't see the halo.

TAW. I prayed all night. *(Roma thinks through that, rises in place and again studies Taw's face carefully, then extends her right hand.)*

ROMA. Then you don't need me. *(Waits.)* Goodbye, Taw. I can wish you good luck. *(Taw sits on a moment, then realizes she has been dismissed. She rises but declines to take Roma's hand.)*

TAW. You don't want to help?

ROMA. I think I have — all I honestly can. I can't improve on your plans and God's. *(Waits.)* You need any cash?

TAW. No ma'm. I'm kin to some openhanded people.

ROMA. Your aunt in Raleigh?

TAW. Many more, many places.

ROMA. Then you'll be wanting to head on to them. *(Moves past Taw toward the door again, opens it, stands there waiting with a smile. Taw is incredulous but keeps her face steady. With no touch or wave, she moves past Roma and out of the house.)*

ACT TWO

Scene 1

The same day, three in the afternoon. Genevieve Slappy, still in her house-robe, works at a large sewing machine in her front room. Materials are strewn about her; she is plainly adept and proceeds intently for a moment. At the end of her seam, she faces the audience.

GENEVIEVE. I'm the youngest property-owner I know — this whole house is mine. Mother left it to me when my brother Dillard and his big family were jammed in a one-story matchbox on the hot side of town. She hoped I would sit here, quiet — renting rooms the rest of my life — and forget Wayne Watkins and the dream of marriage.

I don't understand. She and my father were happy together as any two ducks on a deep warm pond. Many times as a child I woke in the night and heard them laughing in the dark down the hall. But when my father died, Mother — young as she was — just started shrinking day by day till the night she vanished.

Or so I recall it. She never warned me off men or low-rated love till the evening she left us. Then that night, in the back bedroom, I took in her supper; and she said "Sit still while I tell you what's true." I sat by her knees, and she said "Stop waiting by the door like a dog." I said "Beg your pardon?" She shut her eyes and waited and then said "I'll pardon you when you can stand alone."

I'd been walking unaided from the age of ten months — it bowed my knees slightly — and I reminded her of that. I also mentioned how she'd leaned on Papa those twenty-eight good years. She didn't give an inch but turned her face to the wall, the picture she'd painted as a girl — of buffalo — and she said "Then I can't pardon you tonight, can I?"

I laughed "No ma'm. Wait till breakfast tomorrow." And she died before day — leaving me all this, as I said: *(Gestures around.*) my life. So she hoped anyhow. She may yet prevail. It *is* a strong house — heartwood beams and floors.

Scene 2

Immediately after, Genevieve continues sewing and does not hear Taw's first knock; but at the second knock, she goes, opens quickly, leads Taw to a littered daybed and motions her down.

TAW. You're busy.

GENEVIEVE. On my world-famed trousseau. Believe me, it can wait. *(Taw sits. Genevieve returns to her sewing chair.)*

TAW. You were right.

GENEVIEVE. She turned you down?

TAW. And tore me up.

GENEVIEVE. By telling the facts? She's noted for that. You heard what she did when Neal's father died?

TAW. No.

GENEVIEVE. Child, that was all but *radio* news. *(Waits.)* They brought Mr. Avery's corpse to the house in a grand walnut coffin, and everybody gathered that night after supper to pay their respects. Neal was on hand to greet them and sober as a yardstick. But Roma Avery was nowhere in sight.

Everybody knew of course that she and the corpse had barely said "Morning" since Neal was born; so they hung on, hoping she'd finally appear in widow's weeds and some kind of tears. At nine p.m. Roma stalked in in pumps, a teal-blue dress, one strand of pearls and a *serious* screwdriver.

TAW. I won't ask why.

GENEVIEVE. Nobody else did. Miss Roma always explains herself. Straight as a rail, she went to the coffin and unscrewed the little brass plaque on the side. Next she turned to us all, held out the plaque and read the only two words — *At Rest.* Then she said "'At *Rest*'? If any son of a bitch was ever frying in Hell, it's Britt Butler Avery." *(Waits.)* That cleared the mourners in four seconds flat.

TAW. *(Smiles.)* I didn't stay many minutes longer today.

GENEVIEVE. But you said your piece?

TAW. I told her I meant to take Neal off from here.

GENEVIEVE. You never told me one word about that. Take him where, for what?

TAW. Anywhere they have jobs. To clear his slate. To keep us married, like you want us to be.

GENEVIEVE. I wish you'd told me before you saw Roma. I'd have saved you the trip. She could no more visualize Neal going farther than her voice can reach than you'd see yourself as a virgin martyr in the jaws of lions.

TAW. I know that now.

GENEVIEVE. Hush. You don't. And she'll fight you every inch you take. *(Waits.)* Did Neal say he'd leave?

TAW. Neal hasn't said anything clear enough to hear.

GENEVIEVE. Had he talked to his mother anytime today?

TAW. She didn't let on.

GENEVIEVE. He's talked to Porter; you can bet on that.

TAW. I hope not. But you're bound to be right.

GENEVIEVE. Then go beg Porter to ease your way. *(As Taw shakes her head.)* Porter Farwell can tame Neal Avery out of trees. I've seen him do it — out of literal *trees* in the pitch-black winter night and Neal buck naked on the top branch, drunk, stealing mistletoe. Neal used to strip a lot.

TAW. Genevieve, I'd gladly eat fire and die for Neal; but God on His chair can't force me to beg my life and my husband's from Porter Farwell.

GENEVIEVE. Nothing wrong with Porter.

TAW. That a gun wouldn't cure.

GENEVIEVE. Or a wife and ten children.

TAW. Which is roughly as likely as kittens from cows.

GENEVIEVE. Taw, Porter is kind. His head may be a little lost in the mist, but he'd give you the last drop of water on Earth.

TAW. And hold your husband in his other hand.

GENEVIEVE. *(Nods.)* He's sworn to Neal.

TAW. In whose church please?

GENEVIEVE. Oh just in *life*, from the cradle up. They've known each other forever, barring four days — Porter's four days older. No other friend's meant as much to either one.

TAW. Friendships need to end in childhood, along with mumps and five-year diaries. *(Genevieve moves to her sewing machine and sits. She carefully pedals a short burst of stitching. Then she faces Taw.)*

GENEVIEVE. I thought we were friends — that we helped each other with our glorious lives. But since we aren't, or so you claim, then I'm free now to say what I've thought about you all day — you are out of your mind.

Taw, I *live* for a few friends and one shaky boy — Wayne Watkins — that won't even ask for my hand. You sound like Roma Avery, chaining people to you and gnawing their bones.

TAW. You notice I'm alone though.

GENEVIEVE. Damned right — and may be alone from here on out. People in general aren't in it for the pain. If you want company — Neal's or mine or a bobcat's — you got to let up.

TAW. Starting how?

GENEVIEVE. If I tell you — and I *know* — I'll be wasting good air.

TAW. Maybe not. I may be scared.

GENEVIEVE. Good — it's way past time. Listen. Roma turned you down. She'll never change course; and she'll have Neal up at her house right now, laying down her law and cutting at you. You need to find Porter — tell him truly what's happened and beg him to help you save your life, if you want this life.

TAW. *(Stands and slowly moves toward the door, then turns.)* I may not want it, if it's hard as this.

GENEVIEVE. It is. Any set of good eyes sees that by age five. *(Waits.)* I'll help you pack or I'll wait here and pray. But really, I can't keep talking like this. It's ruining my whole outlook on life, and I don't want it ruined. I'm a loving soul with too much to face. *(Taw nods and leaves. Genevieve slowly returns to work.)*

Scene 3

Three forty-five in the afternoon. Porter Farwell steps from Avery's Clothing, where he and Neal work, into the back alley.

There among wood packing crates, Taw is waiting for him.

Porter is genuinely puzzled.

PORTER. *Taw* — Jake said it was you, but I barely believed him. Come on inside.

TAW. I can't see Neal.

PORTER. Neal's up at his mother's.

TAW. Please let me speak here.

PORTER. *(Smiles.)* You giving me the Gettysburg Address or Washington's Farewell to the Infant Nation?

TAW. I'm asking you to help me and my husband.

PORTER. Neal — *that* husband?

TAW. I'm too tired to joke. I hoped you'd be.

PORTER. I seem to have got a second wind after lunch. *(Waits.)* It was a long night.

TAW. Second wind is all I'm asking you for, for me and Neal both — or *first* wind truly. I'm not sure you ever gave us first wind.

PORTER. It wasn't mine to give. I gave the groom *away*, remember? You took over there.

TAW. You've had him most nights.

PORTER. *(Smiles.)* Way less than half. Neal's old enough to vote.

TAW. That's the reason I'm in this back alley now, eating crow by the handful — to ask you to take your hat out of the ring. Stop running for Neal. *(Porter moves to a packing crate, politely motions Taw to another, then seats himself carefully. Taw remains*

36

standing.)

PORTER. My little office with Neal is for life — private dog-catcher maybe or municipal joke.

TAW. Not *so,* Porter. There's no more future in you and Neal, sleeping drunk by the road, than in peace on Earth. *(Porter thinks, then suddenly rises and moves toward Taw. Taw holds her ground. Porter goes back and sits. Then at last Taw sits.)*

PORTER. You turned gypsy on us?

TAW. Sir?

PORTER. You foreseeing things?

TAW. It doesn't take a gypsy or a telescope, just a set of eyes that have watched the world.

PORTER. And you've watched long enough to see all friend-ships fade and die?

TAW. *(Nods.)* I'm an orphan, Porter.

PORTER. That's a famous fact. You could do lecture tours — Little Taw in the Snow.

TAW. *(Waits.)* I pity you — the life you'll have.

PORTER. You foresee that too?

TAW. Right to the end — a dark rented room, an old man lonesome as a rock in the sky.

PORTER. *(Waits, then laughs.)* I'd better start taking more exercise. I'll need extra strength, just standing upright with no helping hand. You of course foresee strong arms under you?

TAW. If you let Neal loose.

PORTER. You can't think *I'm* what's holding Neal?

TAW. Who else is in sight?

PORTER. His mother, his mind — all it dreams to do.

TAW. Neal Avery's mind is promised to me. I've got the signed oath — most people call it a marriage certificate.

PORTER. *(Smiles.)* I signed it too. *(Taw looks puzzled.)* As best man. Remember? The best man's the witness.

TAW. Then the best man leaves. That's his last duty.

PORTER. Where does he go? *(Waits, then laughs.)* What am I meant to do?

TAW. Tell Neal to leave town — now, with his wife.

PORTER. Using what for money? — he works right here.

TAW. We're both strong as bears.

PORTER. Not Neal.

TAW. Then me — *me*, Porter: I'm one strong soul. I'll work for us both.

PORTER. While Neal turns to putty.

TAW. In *my* hands, at least — his legal mate. No, Neal's meant to be far stronger than you guess. He needs to be more than a lovable smile. I know; I've lain down beside him enough. He's waiting to find his own path and walk.

PORTER. And you're his guide through the underbrush?

TAW. The one he chose.

PORTER. He told me he had till sundown to choose.

TAW. *(Waits.)* He has. But now I've begged you to help. Want me to crawl on my knees right here? *(Half-starts to kneel.)*

PORTER. *(Stops her with a wave.)* You didn't really hear my question, Taw. What am *I* meant to do?

TAW. *(Waits.)* Hunt you up your own grown life. *(Porter thinks, laughs a short low note, then rises. He moves toward the door, then turns.)*

PORTER. You more or less ruined my afternoon, but leave — I'll do the little I can.

TAW. He'll listen to you.

PORTER. *(Smiles.)* He never has yet. You never understood — Neal Avery knows what he wants and takes it. Neal Avery, drunk, is clearer than most Baptist preachers at dawn. *(Through the following, moves slowly toward the door.)*

The night before he married you, Neal drove me out toward the river; and we somehow got lost — in country we'd known every day of our lives. So we left the car and struck out walking on the sandy road. Neal said he could smell water straight ahead. I told him he was crazy; we'd get lost deeper.

He said "Stay with me. This is my last exhibit." I said "What of?" And Neal said "Powers I'm losing tomorrow." I walked on beside him; and in maybe half an hour we were wading in river water, warm on our knees.

On the way back home — it was already day — I asked Neal why he was losing powers. He said "I thought I'd be a human for a while." I said "Then who have I known up till now?" And he said "Your guess is good as mine, but it's been grand fun."

TAW. *(Gently.)* I ended his fun? Cost him his powers?

PORTER. He never said that.

TAW. You just did.

PORTER. I told you a story.

TAW. With a moral at the end.

PORTER. I stopped short of that.

TAW. Spell it out, Porter. You're the only one *knows.*

PORTER. Step back. *(Taw takes a step back.)* Not from me — I meant Neal.

TAW. *(Looks around quickly.)* I'm on Mars now. I can barely *see* Neal, he's so far off.

PORTER. *(Shakes his head slowly.)* You're right at his throat.

TAW. It's where I belong — *(Waits to calm.)* Keep talking please.

PORTER. You're the trained talker. *(But then he steps closer; Taw waits in place.)* See, Neal needs help just to draw his next breath. He can't be by himself long enough to shave. But he never heard those marriage vows, never guessed they were laws. You've told him now but he needs more time.

TAW. He's had a long year.

PORTER. Not really. Believe me — he's had just today, since you struck him at dawn.

TAW. But *you* understood every vow we took, the instant we spoke.

PORTER. *(Nods.)* I did — I'm sorry.

TAW. *(Waits to comprehend his concession, then moves a short step closer.)* Now what?

PORTER. For who?

TAW. Neal and me, you, his mother.

PORTER. Let me just speak for Neal. This is Neal's home, Taw — pull him up, he'll die. All his roots are here, all the lights that show him he's thriving and useful. Give him air and ground-room; he may well grow.

TAW. He's no plant, Porter. I'm not a plant doctor. Prescribe for the *humans.*

PORTER. *(Waits.)* Same prescription — air and room. *(Slowly turns to the door.)* Of course Porter Farwell may land behind bars, practicing medicine without a state license. *(Taw stays in*

place but gives a small wave.)
TAW. We could bail you out.
PORTER. Start saving-up now. *(Nods goodbye and opens the door.)*
TAW. Thank you, hear? *(Porter watches her calmly but neither moves nor speaks. Taw waits a moment, then hurries away.)*

Scene 4

Immediately after. Porter shuts the door, returns to the crates and faces the audience.

PORTER. In a town this size, everybody's known your family since the Seven Years' War; so you have to live most of your life in code — little signs and fables for the kind and wise, not actual touch or plain true words. That's been all right by me most times; it keeps you from having to make up your mind too fast, or ever.

For years you can walk around some strong magnet and never ask why or be told to explain. Then when you least expect it, somebody you've known from the dark of the womb will step up and reach for the trunk of your life and shake it like a cyclone, and you'll shed your apples in full public view.

It happened to me my first year in high school, fourteen years old — English class, of course. Miss Speed Brickhouse went round the room asking everybody what they hoped to be; and everybody answered some sensible way — storekeeper, bank teller, practical nurse. Then she called on me — "Porter, what's your plan?"

I was already helping at Avery's Store — Neal and I on Saturdays — and I figured I'd sell men's clothing for life. But what I said was what slipped out. To Miss Speed's withered face, and twenty-six children vicious as bats, I said "I hope to be a lighthouse for others."

Miss Speed tried to save the day by saying the church was the noblest career, but everybody knew she was wrong, and they *howled* — right on through Commencement three whole years later.

40

I found the strength to hold my ground though, and I never explained. I knew I'd found, and told, the truth — a real light, for safety, in cold high seas.

Not for *others* though; I lied in that — just for Neal Avery, the one I'd long since chosen as being in special need and worthy of care. I may well have failed.

Scene 5

Four o'clock in the afternoon. Roma Avery's kitchen. Roma is finishing icing a cake.

Neal enters briskly.

Roma comes from the counter with her cake and sets it at one end of the table.

Neal sits, looks toward the cake and touches it but does not taste his finger.

ROMA. Let me know when you're ready. (*Neal nods but does not meet her eyes. Roma sits at his left. Finally Neal turns and studies her.*)
NEAL. You're in one piece — no obvious abrasions. (*Roma looks puzzled.*) On the phone you sounded like enema-time at the St. Louis Zoo.
ROMA. When were you in St. Louis?
NEAL. In my dreams.
ROMA. Then maybe you and Taw can go there soon.
NEAL. Why so?
ROMA. Taw said you were leaving. She paid me a visit with that little news.
NEAL. News to me.
ROMA. Then your wife flat lied.
NEAL. Mother, Taw's failings don't include deceit. You misunderstood.
ROMA. Enlighten me please.
NEAL. Taw thinks this whole place is bad for me — her and

me.

ROMA. Where would be good?

NEAL. Where she and I could be together more.

ROMA. What's stopping you from clamping your pink limbs together sixteen hours a day?

NEAL. *(Laughs but waits, then not facing Roma.)* That'll be my private concern, please ma'm.

ROMA. You leaving here would concern *me* deeply. You're my right hand in business; you're my one blood child.

NEAL. Porter runs the store; I'm just the handshaker, the boy with the grin. And I'm not sure I ever volunteered to be your child.

ROMA. *(Smiles.)* Of course you did. In Heaven little unborn babies are shown snapshots of lonely women; they're given plenty time to study each face. Then they choose who they like.

NEAL. And are stuck with the choice? *(Smiles.)* Mother for life?

ROMA. Life and beyond. Does marriage offer that?

NEAL. Jesus said nobody gets married in Heaven.

ROMA. Which is why it's Heaven. But he didn't say people forget their mothers.

NEAL. Didn't say redheads get in half-price either. *(Roma cuts a slice of cake, extends it to Neal. Neal shakes his head No. Roma sets the plate in the absolute center of the table before them.)*

ROMA. Leave tonight. I'll support you ninety days.

NEAL. *Whoa —*

ROMA. Asheville. Chattanooga. Hell, Salt Lake City.

NEAL. And you'll come behind us, to balance the books?

ROMA. *(Smiles.)* I'll sit in this house and eat thin slices of my own strong heart till nobody's left still standing but me.

NEAL. After that?

ROMA. I'll join you in eternity, angel.

NEAL. *(Laughs, reaches for the slice of cake and tastes it.)* I'll make you a serious proposition. *(Waits as Roma leans forward.)* I shoot myself late tonight by the river. You bury me neatly in my pin-striped suit. Then, with no harsh word, you give Taw ten thousand dollars cash. She'll leave. Your path'll be clear. Taw can start over fresh.

ROMA. *(Waits.)* Would she sign a paper? — no further claim

on me?

NEAL. *(Eats more cake.)* Take me seriously for once.

ROMA. I do. I accept your proposition.

NEAL. *(Laughs.)* Want to oil the gun? You can hold it maybe. I can fire it with my toes.

ROMA. I'd have a long wait. *(When Neal looks puzzled.)* You'd never do it. *(Waits.)* You love the world.

NEAL. *(Laughs.)* What makes you think that?

ROMA. Love it far more than I or your father. I've known it almost since you were born, when I realized everyone that saw you loved you. I was jealous at first — so few loved me — and then I saw the reason: no virtue of yours; you just loved the world; you begrudged it nothing. Your kind is so rare, people love you on sight.

NEAL. I can thank you, Mother, but say you're wrong. I'm just a regular no-count boy that won't be a man but wants a man's pay — a good cook to curl up next to at night.

ROMA. Taw said there wasn't much curling up.

NEAL. *(Smiles.)* Since I love the whole world, I can't be partial to any one creature.

ROMA. Don't leave here, Neal.

NEAL. They were busy at the store. I better get back.

ROMA. You know what I mean.

NEAL. No ma'm. But I know you'll spell it out for me right now — slowly, in English. *(Raises both hands as if to lead a band.)*

ROMA. You leave and I'll die.

NEAL. I believe you.

ROMA. And you still mean to leave?

NEAL. I haven't said that.

ROMA. But you will, by dark.

NEAL. *(Standing in place.)* You're the prophetess, Mother. I'm just the boy that loves here-and-now.

ROMA. Then I'm as here-and-now as anything else. *(Neal moves to her, slowly leans to kiss the top of her head. Then he rises and stands still a moment before he leaves.)*

Scene 6

Immediately after. Roma stays at the table and faces the audience.

ROMA. Till the day he died, my father was the thing I thought loved me. He was young — nineteen the year I was born — and he seldom spoke ten words a day; so he never *told* me, never spoke the word: not *love*, not in my hearing at least. That was fine by me. All this talk of mine — my Famous Fountain of Truth — came after he died.

Till I was four I said not a word and almost never cried, and by then Mother'd told the world I was mute. Father didn't seem to worry a bit but rode me everywhere he went, on his broad English saddle, far out in the country — he managed timber for his great-grandfather, who'd known James Madison when he was a boy.

The winter I was four, we were out near the river, in a noon so bright my eyes stayed shut; and Father spoke for the first time in hours. He said "Rome, speak now — this precious instant — or nevermore."

So my eyes clicked open, and I said plainly "Let's just keep going on from here." I meant *Not home. Anywhere else but home,* though Mother was a saint almost beyond doubt.

Father said not a word but spurred us on. I think he obeyed me, I honestly do, till midafternoon. At least we saw trees we'd never passed before, both of us silent as stones, each step.

Then a moment came when I felt him turn back. I knew because I was happy till then; but once that horse turned home at a jog, I broke like a stick — for good, for life. Just two nights later Father died across town at a girl's back door, shot once by her brother in the midst of his heart in dark thick as fur.

Next morning I commenced normal speech, no tears, with nobody I much cared to address — not then or since. In the last twenty years, I've enjoyed Neal of course. Father shows in his eyes sometimes, in the dusk. *(Slowly strokes her eyes.)*

Scene 7

Four-thirty in the afternoon, Avery's Clothing. Porter, with a tape measure round his neck, sorts trousers on a table. Another table, bare, is nearby.

Neal enters.

PORTER. You seem to be alive — *(Neal extends his arms, then his legs, as if to check them.)*
NEAL. Barely, I guess.
PORTER. And you calmed your mother?
NEAL. Jesus, with morphine, wouldn't calm Mother. Taw paid her a visit.
PORTER. Taw's had a full day. She honored *me.*
NEAL. When?
PORTER. Just now, in the alley. She wouldn't come in.
NEAL. *(Sits on the bare table.)* What did she want?
PORTER. Perfect peace, perfect light.
NEAL. Porter, tell the truth.
PORTER. Swear to God. I just changed the wording. *(Waits.)* She wants me to beg you to do her will.
NEAL. You promise you would?
PORTER. I think so, yes.
NEAL. *(Waits, then harshly.)* Go to it. Beg.
PORTER. Keep your word to Taw.
NEAL. Recite me the vows.
PORTER. Sir?
NEAL. The marriage vows — you were there by me, weren't you?
PORTER. *(Smiles.)* "Till death do us part."
NEAL. Then what about Mexico — high snow in August?
PORTER. Take her there, sure. She's earned the view.
NEAL. It was our idea — yours and mine: today, off and on for years. You backing out now?
PORTER. It was no idea — just our latest hangover. I sell

45

britches, Neal, and gloves and socks. I will till I die. You and I've got the future of a keg of drowned cats.

NEAL. You always said that friendship outlasted women and rocks.

PORTER. I doubt it now.

NEAL. Since Taw's little visit?

PORTER. Since the day you saw her by the horseshoe pit.

NEAL. I won the match, Porter. Taw didn't stop me. No girl ever has. I can look and still throw.

PORTER. You weren't just looking that day; I saw you.

NEAL. I was also eating six brown-sugar pies and winning a sack race — you see that too?

PORTER. *(Nods.)* And drinking two full jars of raw apple brandy. But Taw Sefton changed you for good, at first sight.

NEAL. I thought she looked good; I could tell she was smart.

PORTER. You thought she was God, with an angel squad.

NEAL. Get serious.

PORTER. Previous times I'd watched you skate fast figures round two dozen girls and plow home at daybreak, not even fazed. But Taw struck you like a pig-iron truck. When I drove you home, you were still burning high.

NEAL. She did look fine. And she talked plain sense, with no mean edge. Seemed not to think I was any big savior.

PORTER. She *chose* you, Neal. I watched her do it.

NEAL. She gave me two minutes — she was with Tim Page.

PORTER. That was all she needed. She knew on the spot. Tim Page might as well have been in Cuba.

NEAL. It did move fast. *(Waits.)* Now we're *stopped* — hell, pasted on the windshield.

PORTER. Crank it, boy. It's your vehicle and you're at the wheel. But slower this time.

NEAL. *(Waits.)* Climb back in.

PORTER. Sir?

NEAL. You. I need you. Let's clear out. Now.

PORTER. For how long?

NEAL. A few days. Ten years.

PORTER. With Taw in the middle?

NEAL. She'd go her own way.

PORTER. Your mother would too, straight to the Law. We'd come back in irons — embezzler's jail.

NEAL. Tell me one thing plain — you don't want to go anywhere but here?

PORTER. No I don't. *(Neal waits, then stands and takes three steps to leave.)* Neal, God and you know I'd go with you to Asia — on yak-back-through-hail — if there seemed any chance we'd end up glad.

NEAL. We'd be taking a *trip*, the sky wouldn't fall.

PORTER. On me it would. Dumb old me. See, everything I know lives here. I might not know how to breathe elsewhere.

NEAL. *(Points to his eyes.)* Keep trusting *me*. I'll teach you to breathe and far more, friend — all grades of wonders. *(Waits.)* We'll be free, Lord Jesus!

PORTER. No, I'm Porter Farwell — always will be.

NEAL. You'd be Porter *free*.

PORTER. *(Waits.)* I'm free right now, of all but you.

NEAL. *(Waits in place, facing Porter frankly.)* Wasn't that a choice?

PORTER. *(Nods.)* Made by me.

NEAL. Then I can't help you, can I?

PORTER. *(Waits.)* Yes. Go to Taw — by dark. Soon now. *(Neal shakes his head slowly — refusal? disbelief? — and leaves. Porter takes his tape measure and carefully calculates the length of his left arm.)*

Scene 8

Six-thirty in the evening, Taw and Neal's room. Taw is setting two places at the center table; and behind on the stove, supper is cooking. She has changed into her newest dress, severe but becoming. At the foot of the bed, her two suitcases stand packed and ready.

Genevieve, bearing a large dish, knocks.

47

Taw balks before answering.

Genevieve opens the unlocked door.

GENEVIEVE. I'm not Neal Avery but I *can* cook beans. These are navy beans; they can sail you to Spain.

TAW. I may not need to go farther than Raleigh but thank you, Gen. *(Genevieve moves to the oven, puts in the beans. Taw continues table-setting.)*

GENEVIEVE. I see you're expecting a guest anyhow.

TAW. Is my husband a guest? *(Smiles.)* Well yes, I'm setting the table on faith. And cooking enough for the Elks' Lodge banquet.

GENEVIEVE. *(Moves toward the door.)* Call me if you need another mouth to help eat. I'll be upstairs praying.

TAW. For what?

GENEVIEVE. You and Neal, me and Wayne, all lonely souls.

TAW. Wayne's not dropping by?

GENEVIEVE. It's the night he cuts his daddy's hair; that can take several days.

TAW. The old fellow's bald.

GENEVIEVE. No, that's his step-dad; his real dad's shaggy as a cold Shetland pony. *(Opens the door.)*

TAW. Please sit down.

GENEVIEVE. I'd be in the way.

TAW. I'm not too sure there *is* a way.

GENEVIEVE. Play like there is. That's my big philosophy; it got me this far. *(Again Taw beckons her to come back and sit. Genevieve goes to the chair.)*

TAW. I'm a terrible truster. If your parents die on you —

GENEVIEVE. *(Her hand in the air, a brake on Taw.)* Don't tell me again; I'm scared enough.

TAW. You'll be all right; both of us will.

GENEVIEVE. People die every day, flat howling lonesome.

TAW. There are far worse things than a lone life.

GENEVIEVE. Name one.

TAW. *(Waits.)* Watching children starve.

GENEVIEVE. Or letting go of a child good as Neal. *(Points.)* I see those bags.

TAW. I'm packed to leave if Neal says leave — with him or alone. I'm ready for supper if that's the plan. You and Porter both said *Let go*.

GENEVIEVE. You truly saw Porter? I bet *he* was kind.

TAW. He said *Let go*, the same as you.

GENEVIEVE. *(Shakes her head No.)* I said start trying to like Neal's nature, the one God gave —

TAW. Porter said I might hold him if I just surrendered. I never once thought I had any guns.

GENEVIEVE. You're armed all right.

TAW. I guess I can try to blind my eyes to some of his ways. But what I suspect is, the *sight* of me hurts him — just me in this room where he comes to rest.

GENEVIEVE. Wayne thinks I'm a damned federal marshal with bloodhounds, handcuffs and convict stripes. But I'll wait him out. One day he'll wake up and see I'm the person that loves his eyes and how he walks and will be true to him in any dark corner.

TAW. You've killed your pride. Mine is still so strong I can barely bend down.

GENEVIEVE. Pride's a sin, in all churches, Taw. Course I never had much. I *wait* a lot and it ruins my posture — I slouch through fights.

TAW. Not I. *(Extends both arms.)* I'm covered with mine and Neal's scars.

GENEVIEVE. *(Actually looks at both Taw's arms.)* Yours don't show.

TAW. I know where they are. I can't forget —

GENEVIEVE. Forget. *Now*. Catch a case of amnesia. Enter life fresh as a rose, this instant.

TAW. *(Smiles.)* A rose with the blight —

GENEVIEVE. The world loves a rose. *(Neal has approached. Now he knocks at the door. Genevieve looks to Taw, mouths the name Neal and rises to leave. Taw firmly motions her down, then goes and opens the door. Neal is empty-handed.)*

TAW. Lost your key? It was open anyhow.

NEAL. I thought I'd play the gent for once.

TAW. I'll remember you that way then — many thanks. *(Ges-*

tures him in.)

NEAL. You're certain now?

TAW. It's where we can talk till the rent expires. The landlady's here —

GENEVIEVE. *(Rising.)* And outward bound.

NEAL. *(Gravely.)* Sit down, stay still, I brought you a message. *(Neal moves toward Genevieve, searching his pockets. Genevieve looks increasingly anxious. Finally Neal throws up his hands in failure.)* It was nothing but a wire.

GENEVIEVE. A *wire?* Who's dead?

NEAL. From Wayne.

GENEVIEVE. *Wayne?*

NEAL. You're developing a problem with your eardrums, Gen. I said "From Wayne" — your aging beau. As I passed Western Union just now, they asked me to bring it; tipped me ten cents — here. *(Reaches for a dime and hands it to Genevieve.)*

GENEVIEVE. *(Slaps his arm aside.)* Neal, you owe me a whole world more than a thin silver dime. Where is Wayne and what in God's name does he say?

NEAL. You assume I took the liberty of reading a private dispatch?

GENEVIEVE. Wires are public property. How far has he gone? Is he under arrest?

NEAL. *(Removes the wire from an inside pocket, opens it slowly and reads precisely.)* "Wheeling, West Virginia, 1:30 p.m." *(Waits.)* "Up here suddenly with Dad and Dave. Will you marry me Friday if I get home safe? Yours cordially, Wayne." *(Hands over the wire.)*

GENEVIEVE. *(Studies it well, then crushes it in her palm.)* Cordially? They're bound to be drunk.

TAW. Who is Dave?

GENEVIEVE. Mr. Watkins' dog — the one that can sing.

TAW. I hope he can drive; those mountain roads are instant death.

GENEVIEVE. Of course they are. What else would Fate hold for Genevieve Slappy?

NEAL. Shall we join in prayer?

GENEVIEVE. No. *(Waits.)* Neal, is one single word of this true?

(Neal silently raises his right hand — an oath.) You somehow made this whole thing up. Taw, do you believe this fool?

TAW. Forging a wire's a federal offense.

GENEVIEVE. That never stopped Neal.

NEAL. Gen, trust your best friend. Step on upstairs; you'll get a surprise.

GENEVIEVE. *(To Neal.)* I'm in serious pain. What's true in all this?

NEAL. What I just said. Go sit by your hearth; your reward's on the way.

GENEVIEVE. And it's not bad news?

NEAL. Not for you, no ma'm. *(Genevieve stands and heads for the door; then looks back, incredulous.)* Have I ever lied to you?

GENEVIEVE. Just ten times a day since we met in first grade.

NEAL. I'm not lying now. Go in peace; live to thank me.

GENEVIEVE. *(Opens the door.)* Taw, those beans should be warm by now.

TAW. Thank you, Gen. Keep me posted; I'll do the same.

GENEVIEVE. *(Nods.)* Call the Law if I scream.

NEAL. Absolutely.

GENEVIEVE. Not you, fool. Taw, call the true *Law* if I yell murder.

TAW. *(Raising her hand.)* Cross my heart. *(Genevieve leaves. Neal moves to lock the door.)* Leave it unlocked please.

NEAL. You expecting somebody?

TAW. I guess not, no. *(Neal turns the key, then walks to the table. Points to the ceiling.)* You didn't lie to her?

NEAL. I forged the wire but she'll be happy soon. *(As Taw frowns.)* I saw Wayne buying a diamond just now, the size of a gnat — for sweet Genevieve. *(Waits.)* May I rest my feet?

TAW. Help yourself. Sit down. *(Taw moves to the stove and continues to work. After he stands in the midst, seeming lost, Neal walks an uncertain path toward the Morris chair. He stands and regards it like a new-found place; then he seems to measure it with slow gestures. None of his actions is strained or comic; he has no sense of entertaining Taw. She is gone from his mind. Finally he sits, leans well back and shuts his eyes. Taw goes on cooking, adjusting the table settings, pouring two glasses of cool water and setting them precisely by each of their places. Throughout she glances nervously at Neal till at last she cannot bear the silence.)* Neal, are you eating here? *(Neal makes a long deep sound — agreement? Taw steps up behind the sofa, leans over; she wants to smile but cannot trust herself, not to mention trusting Neal.)* Will I ever know?

NEAL. *(Eyes still shut.)* If I ever get back. *(The dreamy words half-startle Taw; she withdraws in silence and stands by the table.)*

TAW. From where; where are you?

NEAL. *(Very slow and distant.)* Way out in what may just be a dream. Moving, moving —

TAW. *(Quietly but with gathering force.)* Move gently. *(Waits.)* Move, Neal. Come on.

NEAL. I'm flying, girl.

TAW. Your own private plane? *(Starts moving bowls of food to the table.)*

NEAL. I think it's — sure: my private *arms.*

TAW. *(Still stocking the table.)* You must be hungry — are you strong enough to make it? Can I guide you in? *(Neal waits a long moment, then rolls to his left side, faces the audience and opens his eyes. Throughout what follows, Taw moves between final adjustments at the table and furtive trips to lean toward Neal and test the truth or fiction of his dream.)*

NEAL. I'm ten years old. The other children hate me, and I start to run. We're on a big ledge of a hill, steep sides. They're about to catch me; they've grabbed my shirttail. But I run the last step over the ledge and fall through space toward a sharp rock valley. The children yell "We're sorry. Come back."

I wish I could; I always loved them. But I'm bound to die. Then my arms stretch out on the wind rushing by. And — God! — I rise fifty yards in a sweep before I level off and glide. I'm scared cold-stiff but I flap my arms, and this time I understand I've learned to fly.

The sun breaks out — there's been a lot of mist — and natural as sleep, I'm climbing and banking and looping-the-loop while all the cruel children line up on the ledge with their mouths wide open and beg me to land and teach them how. I just glide on. *(Shuts his eyes again, then slowly sits up, rubs his face.)*

TAW. *(Stops at the table.)* I thought people loved you.

NEAL. They do, till they know me. Then *they* beg for wings.

TAW. Were you really asleep?

NEAL. Maybe. I wonder. I've dreamed that before, many times through the years. How long was I out?

TAW. Less than three minutes. Maybe you were snoozing. *(Waits.)* The trip make you hungry?

NEAL. I think maybe so.

TAW. *(Gestures to the food.)* It's here then, abundant.

NEAL. *(Stands slowly.)* How much? *(Through the following Neal never smiles or teases. He seems at least a half-new man in his gravity, his voice. Taw is enveloped early in the change; a half-new woman begins to show in her, convinced of her power but generous-hearted.)*

TAW. Food for hundreds.

NEAL. *(Shakes his head.)* How much, if I sit down and eat — how much do I pay?

TAW. You own it already. You well know that.

NEAL. *(Still in place.)* Then you changed the deal.

TAW. Sir?

NEAL. Your morning deal — I would stop my old life and leave here with you.

TAW. I meant I wanted to love you, Neal — in your right mind and *present,* after sundown at least.

NEAL. That simple? Just that?

TAW. *(Nods.)* Where I could see and reach you.

NEAL. I can see you plainly from here. *(Extends a hand as if to touch her, then lets it fall.)*

TAW. Come two steps nearer.

NEAL. *(Takes two large steps.)* See how I've changed?

TAW. *(Studies his face.)* I'd never have known you.

NEAL. Notice the clear eyes, the firm trusty jaw?

TAW. *(Nods.)* A whole new man.

NEAL. *(Holds up a cautionary hand.)* A great deal is hid under these fine clothes.

TAW. And all of it changed?

NEAL. That's your gamble, the risk you take.

TAW. You too. Three-quarters of me is submerged.

NEAL. That sank the Titanic — the buried ice.

TAW. *(Touches her chest.)* I doubt this is ice. *(Neal comes farther toward her and reaches again — still a yard short.)*

NEAL. *(Nods.)* Warm, from here. *(Taw nods. Neal waits, then takes the last steps and touches her chest lightly, just above her breasts.)* You win then? For now?

TAW. *(Shakes her head No.)* I've lost more than you — for good, I suspect.

NEAL. *(Covers her eyes.)* Don't look that far. I might be gone.

TAW. *(Moves her face clear but stands in place.)* The *world* might, Neal — be ashes by midnight, you and me with it.

NEAL. Fine by me.

TAW. Not me.

NEAL. You're young.

TAW. I'm old as the moon — that tired at least.

NEAL. How tired is the moon? *(Then a distant cry. From here to the end, a ritual slowing — no hint of farce. Neal and Taw look to the ceiling.)*

GENEVIEVE'S VOICE. *(Excited but entirely clear.)* Wayne, my darling! It's glorious — and Lord God, look, it fits! *(Waits.)* The answer is Yes — any *day,* and forever. *(Neal, unsmiling, looks down at Taw.)*

NEAL. Do we call the Law?

TAW. *(Facing Neal and also grave.)* She never meant that — I'm all but sure.

NEAL. You take the responsibility then?

TAW. *(Waits.)* I do. *(Still calm and grave, Taw steps back slowly and gestures toward supper. Neal waits a moment, then moves to the table, pulls out Taw's chair and seats her slowly. Then he moves to the opposite chair and sits. Taw passes him a large white bowl. Neal nods and accepts it.)*

PRODUCTION NOTES

The trilogy *New Music* is best seen in sequence, right through on a single afternoon and evening. At its first production, by the Cleveland Play House in 1989, stage time for the three parts was five hours — 92, 92, and 126 minutes. With a half-hour intermission between *August Snow* and *Night Dance*, and a 90-minute pause for dinner before *Better Days*, a full performance takes seven hours.

One fluid set will serve throughout — sparely furnished areas for recurrent rooms and one or two neutral spaces for elsewhere. Genevieve's house and Roma's kitchen, for instance, are constant through *August Snow* and *Night Dance*, with small changes in the eight-year gap. Since *Better Days* is set in Roma's kitchen, with moments in two nearby bedrooms, the kitchen may be subtly enlarged.

Place and time are given as North Carolina in the midst of this century. In the upper South of those years, before wide contact with a larger world, an ancient and prodigal strain of the English language was a birthright to every native. For more than three centuries, its power was lavishly spent by people who often lacked other coinage — for care and loathing, to maim or heal. Mostly they spoke in a constant exchange of story and parable — the appalling heroic tales of one talking species adrift on Earth.

The acts and words of *New Music* start at least in that life-or-death need to face and bend reality with speech. But the aim is not for a polished mirror of a land-locked time. All speech and action hope to move further and find, in one family's long discord, a broadly useful harmony — a new old music and the dance it stirs.

Unless all actors are native to the region, an effort to mimic precise accents is likely to fail. Avoid "stage-Southern" dialects, above all the fake-hillbilly nasal twang so often assumed by strangers — *Whīte īce at a nīce prīce.*

But note each character's private rhythms and the steady build of longer speeches. Ease the -ing endings off participles and adjectives, as most Americans do in conversation. And recall that Southerners often end a sentence with a slight vocal rise, almost a question, in hopes of drawing a listener on.

Try for the implicit whole atmosphere, a close but loose-limbed family of kin and friends who circle in earnest and meet intensely through four decades of a world that changes more rapidly than they. The people differ in origin, station, expressive skills and hopes; but each is formed by the central demand of an old civilization — its codes of courtesy, loyalty, honor and mercy. Recall that most dialects of the South are founded upon the first principle of thoughtful discourse everywhere — *Be as clear and entertaining as truth and brevity allow (and if the truth is boring, don't hesitate to stretch it).*

The South was, and is, a society like others in which hot violence is elaborately hid but coiled to strike — northern Ireland, Sicily, the Middle East. Men and women encounter each other with provisional trust that may instantly flare into danger or death at a hint of trespass or betrayal. But in daily encounters, a harshly raised voice is seldom heard, much less the exasperated irony and insult of many American urban dialects. Here passion, pain or threat is mostly conveyed by clear-eyed eloquence, wit, rhythm, light emphasis and restrained gesture. That struggle to talk, not kill, can lend an armed power to the simplest transaction.

Clothing is of good, though not luxurious, quality. Fashions will be a year or so late. With the exception of Dob Watkins, all are conscious of clothes as another means of diverting and taming the world. Again avoid stereotypes — no white linen suits and string ties for the men, no picture hats or chiffons for the women.

Each play occurs in late summer. In the absence of air conditioning, a towering heat and humidity weigh on speech and action.

Radio was a frequent presence in rooms. So popular band and vocal music of the time — jazz, swing and boogie, romantic ballads, black gospel, blues and rock — may be used to strong effect, provided no meanings are drowned. A striking contrast can be made in *Better Days* between the gentle folk-rock of the sixties and the Vietnam-stained rock that ensued.

PROPERTY LIST

Cotton quilt (Taw)
Towel (Taw)
Comb (Taw)
Water bucket
Dishpan (enamel)
Bowl of eggs
Pot with lid
Radio (Taw, Neal)
Pitcher and bowl for wash basin
Electric fan (Taw, Neal)
Cast iron frying pan (Roma)
Coffee pot (Roma)
3 coffee cups (Roma)
Salt shaker with screw top (Roma)
Pepper shaker (Roma)
2 dinner plates (Roma)
Silverware (Roma):   1 spoon
                     1 knife
                     2 forks

Sugarspoon (Roma)
Sugar bowl (Roma)
Spatula (Roma)
Dish towel (Roma)
Pie plate with peach pie
Silverware (Taw, Neal): 2 spoons
                         3 forks
                         2 knives

Plate (Downtown Cafe)
Water glass (Downtown Cafe)
Silverware (Downtown Cafe):   1 fork
                              1 spoon
                              1 knife

Pocketwatch (Porter)
Book (Roma)
Piece of sewing (Genevieve)

Fabric pieces (Genevieve)
Thread (Genevieve)
Sewing machine (Genevieve)
Iron
Laundry basket with laundry
Radio (Genevieve)
Electric fan (Genevieve)
2 packing crates
Small cake plate (Roma)
Cake plate cover (Roma)
3 napkins (Roma)
Cake server (Roma)
Cake on plate (Roma)
Tape measure (Porter)
Small pile of trousers (Porter)
2 dinner plates (Taw, Neal)
Large dish of beans (Genevieve)
Dime (Neal)
Telegram (Neal)
2 suitcases (Taw)
2 water glasses (Taw, Neal)
Various clothing for closet (Taw)
Cardigan sweater (Taw)
Water pitcher with water
Serving bowl (white)
Cooking spoon
2 napkins (Taw, Neal)
Ham on serving plate
2 serving spoons
Candlestick phone

COSTUME PLOT

Taw Avery
  Dress
  Slip
  Shoes
  Stockings
  Wedding band
  Watch
  Hat
  Purse
  Jacket

Neal Avery
  Sport jacket
  Trousers
  Shirt
  Shoes
  Socks
  Belt
  Necktie
  Hat
  Wedding band
  Watch

Genevieve Slappy
  Housecoat/robe
  Slip/nightgown
  Slippers
  Shoes

Roma Avery
  Bathrobe
  Nightgown
  Slippers
  Hairnet
  Wedding band
  Dress
  Slip
  Stockings
  Corset
  Watch

Porter Farwell
  Suit
  Shirt
  Necktie
  Belt
  Socks
  Shoes
  Hat
  Wrist watch

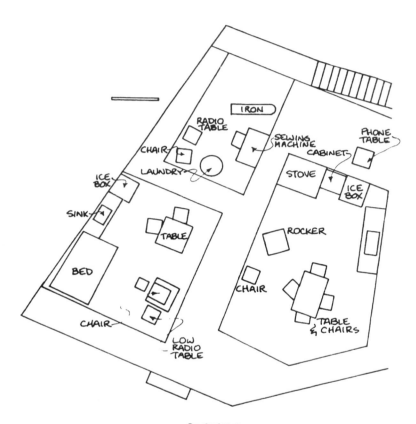

SCENE DESIGN
"AUGUST SNOW"
DESIGNED BY DAN CONWAY
FOR THE CLEVELAND PLAY HOUSE

NEW PLAYS

★ **A LESSON BEFORE DYING by Romulus Linney, based on the novel by Ernest J. Gaines.** An innocent young man is condemned to death in backwoods Louisiana and must learn to die with dignity. "The story's wrenching power lies not in its outrage but in the almost inexplicable grace the characters must muster as their only resistance to being treated like lesser beings." –*The New Yorker*. "Irresistable momentum and a cathartic explosion…a powerful inevitability." –*NY Times*. [5M, 2W] ISBN: 0-8222-1785-6

★ **BOOM TOWN by Jeff Daniels.** A searing drama mixing small-town love, politics and the consequences of betrayal. "…a brutally honest, contemporary foray into classic themes, exploring what moves people to lie, cheat, love and dream. By BOOM TOWN's climactic end there are no secrets, only bare truth." –*Oakland Press*. "…some of the most electrifying writing Daniels has ever done…" –*Ann Arbor News*. [2M, 1W] ISBN: 0-8222-1760-0

★ **INCORRUPTIBLE by Michael Hollinger.** When a motley order of medieval monks learns their patron saint no longer works miracles, a larcenous, one-eyed minstrel shows them an outrageous new way to pay old debts. "A lightning-fast farce, rich in both verbal and physical humor." –*American Theatre*. "Everything fits snugly in this funny, endearing black comedy…an artful blend of the mock-formal and the anachronistically breezy…A piece of remarkably dexterous craftsmanship." –*Philadelphia Inquirer*. "A farcical romp, scintillating and irreverent." –*Philadelphia Weekly*. [5M, 3W] ISBN: 0-8222-1787-2

★ **CELLINI by John Patrick Shanley.** Chronicles the life of the original "Renaissance Man," Benvenuto Cellini, the sixteenth-century Italian sculptor and man-about-town. Adapted from the autobiography of Benvenuto Cellini, translated by J. Addington Symonds. "[Shanley] has created a convincing Cellini, not neglecting his dark side, and a trim, vigorous, fast-moving show." –*BackStage*. "Very entertaining…With brave purpose, the narrative undermines chronology before untangling it…touching and funny…" –*NY Times*. [7M, 2W (doubling)] ISBN: 0-8222-1808-9

★ **PRAYING FOR RAIN by Robert Vaughan.** Examines a burst of fatal violence and its aftermath in a suburban high school. "Thought provoking and compelling." –*Denver Post*. "Vaughan's powerful drama offers hope and possibilities." –*Theatre.com*. "[The play] doesn't put forth compact, tidy answers to the problem of youth violence. What it does offer is a compelling exploration of the forces that influence an individual's choices, and of the proverbial lifelines—be they familial, communal, religious or political—that tragically slacken when society gives in to apathy, fear and self-doubt…" –*Westword*. "…a symphony of anger…" –*Gazette Telegraph*. [4M, 3W] ISBN: 0-8222-1807-0

★ **GOD'S MAN IN TEXAS by David Rambo.** When a young pastor takes over one of the most prestigious Baptist churches from a rip-roaring old preacher-entrepreneur, all hell breaks loose. "…the pick of the litter of all the works at the Humana Festival…" –*Providence Journal*. "…a wealth of both drama and comedy in the struggle for power…" –*LA Times*. "…the first act is so funny…deepens in the second act into a sobering portrait of fear, hope and self-delusion…" –*Columbus Dispatch*. [3M] ISBN: 0-8222-1801-1

★ **JESUS HOPPED THE 'A' TRAIN by Stephen Adly Guirgis.** A probing, intense portrait of lives behind bars at Rikers Island. "…fire-breathing…whenever it appears that JESUS is settling into familiar territory, it slides right beneath expectations into another, fresher direction. It has the courage of its intellectual restlessness…[JESUS HOPPED THE 'A' TRAIN] has been written in flame." –*NY Times*. [4M, 1W] ISBN: 0-8222-1799-6

DRAMATISTS PLAY SERVICE, INC.
440 Park Avenue South, New York, NY 10016 212-683-8960 Fax 212-213-1539
postmaster@dramatists.com www.dramatists.com

NEW PLAYS

★ **THE CIDER HOUSE RULES, PARTS 1 & 2 by Peter Parnell, adapted from the novel by John Irving.** Spanning eight decades of American life, this adaptation from the Irving novel tells the story of Dr. Wilbur Larch, founder of the St. Cloud's, Maine orphanage and hospital, and of the complex father-son relationship he develops with the young orphan Homer Wells. "...luxurious digressions, confident pacing...an enterprise of scope and vigor..." *–NY Times.* "...The fact that I can't wait to see Part 2 only begins to suggest just how good it is..." *–NY Daily News.* "...engrossing...an odyssey that has only one major shortcoming: It comes to an end." *–Seattle Times.* "...outstanding...captures the humor, the humility...of Irving's 588-page novel..." *–Seattle Post-Intelligencer.* [9M, 10W, doubling, flexible casting] PART 1 ISBN: 0-8222-1725-2 PART 2 ISBN: 0-8222-1726-0

★ **TEN UNKNOWNS by Jon Robin Baitz.** An iconoclastic American painter in his seventies has his life turned upside down by an art dealer and his ex-boyfriend. "...breadth and complexity...a sweet and delicate harmony rises from the four cast members...Mr. Baitz is without peer among his contemporaries in creating dialogue that spontaneously conveys a character's social context and moral limitations..." *–NY Times.* "...darkly funny, brilliantly desperate comedy...TEN UNKNOWNS vibrates with vital voices." *–NY Post.* [3M, 1W] ISBN: 0-8222-1826-7

★ **BOOK OF DAYS by Lanford Wilson.** A small-town actress playing St. Joan struggles to expose a murder. "...[Wilson's] best work since *Fifth of July*...An intriguing, prismatic and thoroughly engrossing depiction of contemporary small-town life with a murder mystery at its core...a splendid evening of theater..." *–Variety.* "...fascinating...a densely populated, unpredictable little world." *–St. Louis Post-Dispatch.* [6M, 5W] ISBN: 0-8222-1767-8

★ **THE SYRINGA TREE by Pamela Gien.** Winner of the 2001 Obie Award. A breathtakingly beautiful tale of growing up white in apartheid South Africa. "Instantly engaging, exotic, complex, deeply shocking...a thoroughly persuasive transport to a time and a place...stun[s] with the power of a gut punch..." *–NY Times.* "Astonishing...affecting ...[with] a dramatic and heartbreaking conclusion...A deceptive sweet simplicity haunts THE SYRINGA TREE..." *–A.P.* [1W (or flexible cast)] ISBN: 0-8222-1792-9

★ **COYOTE ON A FENCE by Bruce Graham.** An emotionally riveting look at capital punishment. "The language is as precise as it is profane, provoking both troubling thought and the occasional cheerful laugh...will change you a little before it lets go of you." *–Cincinnati CityBeat.* "...excellent theater in every way..." *–Philadelphia City Paper.* [3M, 1W] ISBN: 0-8222-1738-4

★ **THE PLAY ABOUT THE BABY by Edward Albee.** Concerns a young couple who have just had a baby and the strange turn of events that transpire when they are visited by an older man and woman. "An invaluable self-portrait of sorts from one of the few genuinely great living American dramatists...rockets into that special corner of theater heaven where words shoot off like fireworks into dazzling patterns and hues." *–NY Times.* "An exhilarating, wicked...emotional terrorism." *–NY Newsday.* [2M, 2W] ISBN: 0-8222-1814-3

★ **FORCE CONTINUUM by Kia Corthron.** Tensions among black and white police officers and the neighborhoods they serve form the backdrop of this discomfiting look at life in the inner city. "The creator of this intense...new play is a singular voice among American playwrights...exceptionally eloquent..." *–NY Times.* "...a rich subject and a wise attitude." *–NY Post.* [6M, 2W, 1 boy] ISBN: 0-8222-1817-8

DRAMATISTS PLAY SERVICE, INC.
440 Park Avenue South, New York, NY 10016 212-683-8960 Fax 212-213-1539
postmaster@dramatists.com www.dramatists.com